Footsteps and I

by
Robin Sha(rples)
Illustrated by **Simon Smith**

Hello there!

My name's Robin and I'll be taking you on the first ever Livewires adventure. I've had great fun getting to know the Livewire kids. Tim's written you a letter, so I think I'll let him do the introductions. I hope you'll enjoy getting into the Bible with the Livewires as much as I have—they've certainly kept me on my toes!

Text copyright © Robin Sharples 1996

Illustrations copyright © Simon Smith 1996

The author asserts the moral right to be identified as the author of this work

Published by
The Bible Reading Fellowship
Peter's Way, Sandy Lane West
Oxford OX4 5HG
ISBN 0 7459 3295 9
Albatross Books Pty Ltd
PO Box 320, Sutherland
NSW 2232, Australia
ISBN 0 7324 1552 7

First edition 1996

10 9 8 7 6 5 4 3 2 1 0

All rights reserved

Acknowledgments
Unless otherwise stated, scripture quotations are taken from the Good News Bible published by The Bible Societies/ HarperCollins Publishers Ltd UK © American Bible Society, 1966, 1971, 1976, 1992

A catalogue record for this book is available from the British Library

Printed and bound in Malta by Interprint Limited

An imprint of
The Bible Reading Fellowship

Hi!

You might not have met us before—we're a cool bunch of friends and we call ourselves the Livewires. That's because we love playing with computers and stuff. We usually meet at Annie-log's house 'cos she's the only one of us with a computer!

This is her room and I'm the one by the window, Tim, that's me. Little Ben is on the top bunk and sitting on the bottom bunk is Data, Annie-log's little sister. Annie-log herself is using the keyboard. On the bean bag is Digit, how on earth he manages to see anything with those shades on I have no idea, he never takes them off! Mind you Quartz, she's the one lying on the floor, is always telling me off about my fringe...

So you're wondering why I've written to you? Well it's like this...

One evening, in the middle of winter, there we all were sitting in Annie-log's room. She had just called up the most amazing game from the hard disk when there was a power cut. All the lights went out and everything; it was just totally black. Well you might know what power cuts can do to computers, they can just go barmy. Boot, that's what we call the computer, didn't do anything for a minute... then, before any lights or anything began to work, a tiny white dot appeared on his screen...

it got bigger and bigger...

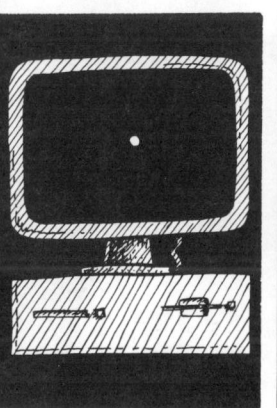 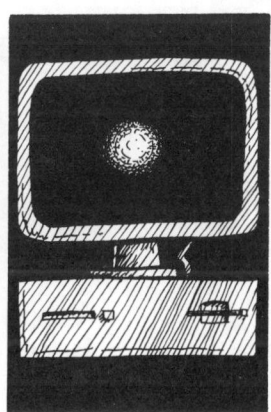 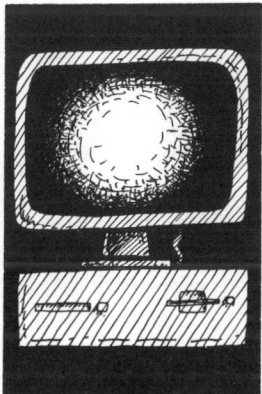 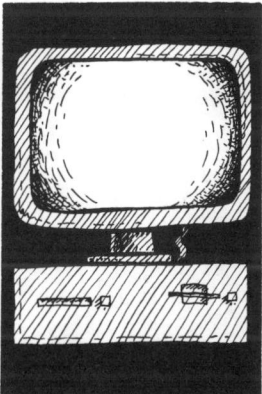

till the whole screen was white...

That's so bright

It hurts my eyes!

Look - WRITING

GENESIS 1:1

"Why don't the lights come back on?"

"Don't panic but I can't feel the bed any more."

The Livewires are in a bit of a difficult spot! Everything is black and they don't seem to be in the bedroom! Boot's screen has changed... now it says...

GENESIS 1.3

"...Then God commanded, 'Let there be light'—and light appeared."

"Wow, what a dump, nothing but puddles and mud!"

"Yeah. Did you hear a voice?"

The Livewires have found themselves right back at the beginning of the Bible.
To help us keep track of the Livewires let's make a special mobile. Start with a muddy world. Cut two circles of card about 10 cm in diameter and draw a really muddy, messy world on one side of each piece. Then glue the two halves together, but put a piece of thread about 30 cm long between them.

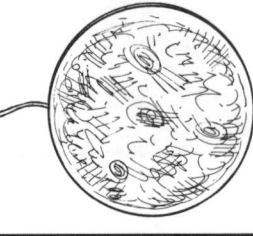

It didn't take the Livewires long to work out what had happened. Data had an idea...

It's about time you made the second part of your mobile. Cut two more circles of card (10 cm across) and draw the sea and sky on each side. Once again glue them together with a piece of thread about 30 cm long between them.

Then God commanded, 'Let the earth produce all kinds of plants, those that bear grain and those that bear fruit'—and it was done.

It is amazing, but whatever happens Data always has something useful up her sleeve...

Let me see

Hey look, there are things growing here!

There, little leaves...

HELP! ... GET ME OUT OF THIS BUSH!!

Things were growing so quickly that the Livewires had to jump about so that they didn't end up in a tangle like Digit!

This time for your mobile cut out eight circles of card and draw four different plants, trees, bushes or flowers. make them a little smaller this time—about 6 cm across.
Glue the circles together with the thread in between as before. You could look outside and copy things that you see. While you do so, think of all the plants that God has made: you might like to say this little prayer:

Dear Lord, thank you for all the beautiful plants, for their colours and scents. Amen

What is Data doing now? Here she is looking into the water with her magnifying glass...

Hey, it's full of things!

Whadaya mean?

Look, all sorts of wriggling things.

Boot, what is going on?

Then God commanded, 'Let the water be filled with many kinds of living beings, and let the air be filled with birds'.

GENESIS 1:20

I'm sure I heard a voice!

Data had seen a few little things in her pool, but all the waters were full of fish, and shrimps and snails and whales and untold numbers of creatures and the air was full of birds. Make some water creature and bird pictures for the mobile ... Meanwhile the Livewires had thought of something.

How long have we been here?

And there was evening and morning the fifth day...

FIVE DAYS !!!!!!!

GENESIS 1 : 23

8

So the Livewires have been at the beginning of the Bible for five days. 'Six days', thought Tychi, looking fed up, 'I don't want to hang around here'.

GENESIS 1:24

Then God commanded, 'Let the earth produce all kinds of animal life: domestic and wild, large and small'... and it was done.

Then God said, 'And now we will make human beings; they will be like us and resemble us'.

GENESIS 1:26

Suddenly there were animals everywhere, cats, rabbits, giraffes and a little dog who would not go away. He chased the Livewires until they came to a garden gate. Through the gate they could see—people!

Cool, that must be Adam and Eve, the first people.

That voice again!

The Livewires can't stay here for ever. It is time to make your last set of pictures for the mobile. Animals this time—and don't forget the people!

Dear God, thank you for the world that you have given me to live in. Help me to enjoy it in such a way that others can enjoy it too. Amen.

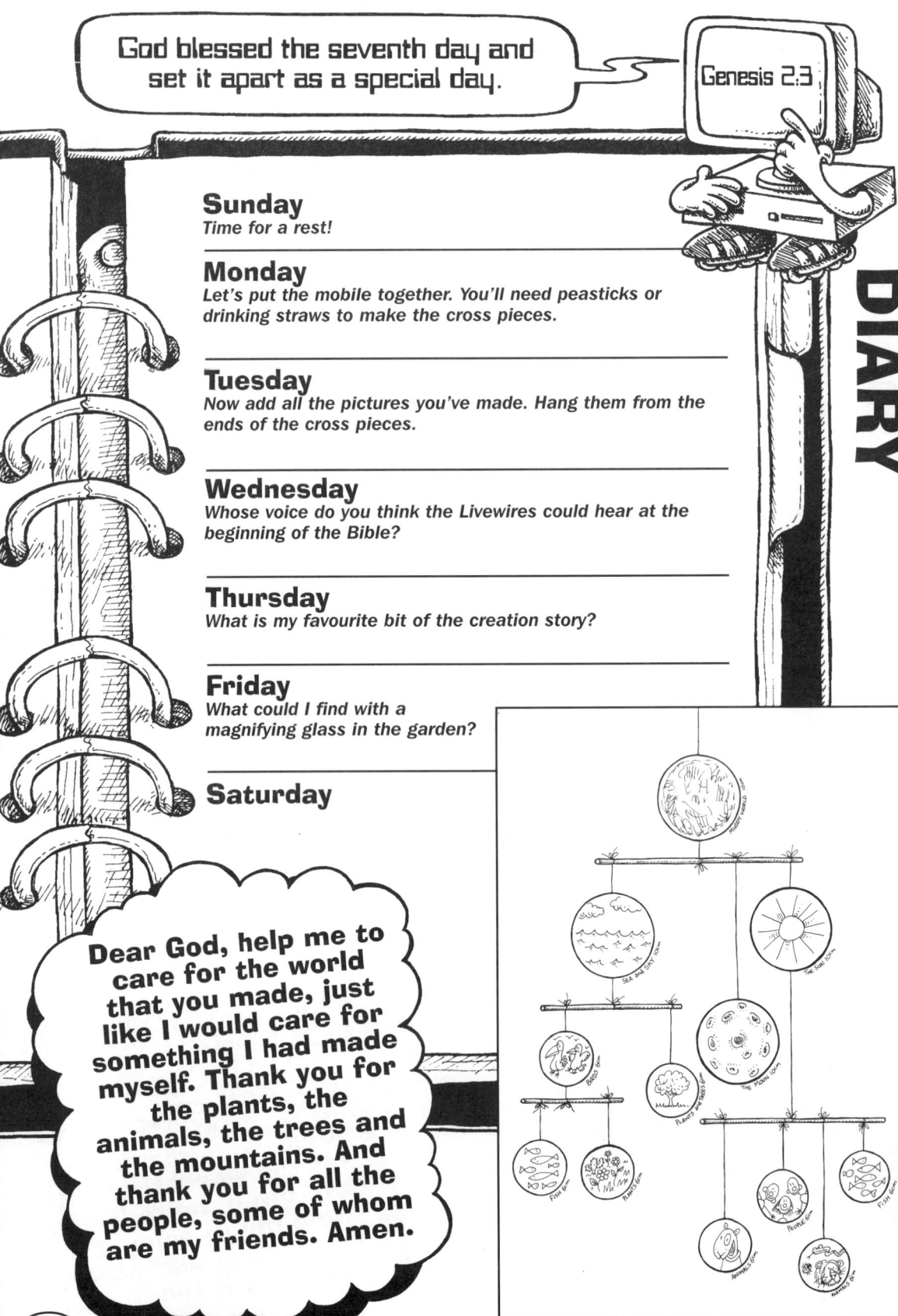

> God blessed the seventh day and set it apart as a special day.
>
> Genesis 2:3

DIARY

Sunday
Time for a rest!

Monday
Let's put the mobile together. You'll need peasticks or drinking straws to make the cross pieces.

Tuesday
Now add all the pictures you've made. Hang them from the ends of the cross pieces.

Wednesday
Whose voice do you think the Livewires could hear at the beginning of the Bible?

Thursday
What is my favourite bit of the creation story?

Friday
What could I find with a magnifying glass in the garden?

Saturday

> Dear God, help me to care for the world that you made, just like I would care for something I had made myself. Thank you for the plants, the animals, the trees and the mountains. And thank you for all the people, some of whom are my friends. Amen.

While Abram was in Canaan there was a bad famine in the land so he went further south, travelling all the way to Egypt. The Livewires followed his footprints all the way there... and all the way back, which is where we catch up with them again, in Canaan. On their walk they had been thinking about what they had heard Abram say to Sarai about promises.

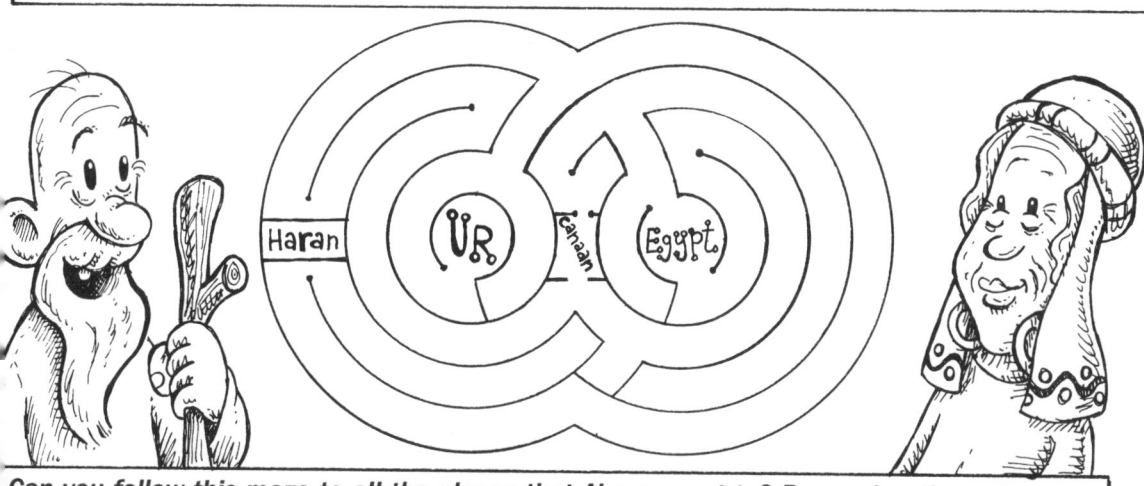

Can you follow this maze to all the places that Abram went to? Remember the order Ur → Haran → Canaan → Egypt → Canaan. Start at Ur...

Promises are tricky things, as you might know. A promise from God is a bit special though. All sorts of things can happen, as the Livewires found out when Annie-log typed a new Bible verse into Boot.

'Your name will no longer be Abram, but Abraham, because I am making you the ancestor of many nations...'

GENESIS 17:5

That's a bit like at a Christening, when a baby is named.

Hang on, Boot hasn't finished.

GENESIS 17:15

'You must no longer call your wife Sarai; from now on her name is Sarah.'

That means 'princess' you know...

13

The Livewires had been following Abram's—I mean Abraham's—footprints for a long time. They were beginning to feel tired, so they asked Boot to find them a place to rest.

GENESIS 18:1

'... Abraham was sitting at the entrance of his tent during the hottest part of the day...'

The Livewires sat down too. They were tired, but even so Data spoke to Abraham...

It's nice to sit down, we've been following you for ages.

Well it's these animals I've got, we have to keep finding grass for them.

Is this a good spot?

It isn't bad, and this land, Canaan, has been promised to my family by God. He said that Sarah is going to be the ancestor of kings.

But she's quite old isn't she?

Yes, we both are and she doesn't believe that she will have a baby. Oh, would you excuse me a minute?

Abraham jumped up as three men walked up to the tent; he spoke to them then hurried off to find Sarah to arrange food...

The Livewires went into the tent to help.

In Old Testament times it was very important to show a welcome to strangers. Do people still do this? When might you not give a welcome to strangers?

The Livewires helped get the food sorted in the tent while Abraham sat under a tree, talking to the men. Sarah listened at the door of the tent. Suddenly she laughed...

Why are you laughing?

Even these men think that I shall have a baby! Everyone is saying it.

HA HA HA

Sarah went out but was soon back through the door, and looking very shaky.

What happened?

I think that it is God out there! He knew that I had laughed!!!

Soon after this Abraham and Sarah moved on; south this time to Kadesh.

The Livewires were not so bothered about following this time, their feet were tired! They were much more interested in a different question...

Did Sarah have a baby?

To find out you'll have to join the Livewires on the next page...

Meanwhile here is a question for you: are you remembering the names of the places that Abraham visited?

Try to find them in this mini-wordsearch:

Canaan, Egypt, Haran, Ur, Shechem, Kadesh

```
A C D E F S T
U A G G D H E
H N U Y A E G
H A R A N C Y
K A D E S H P
K N S H E E T
E G Y P H M T
```

15

Try this name maze. Start at the arrow and try to follow these names in order through it:

Abram, Sarai, Abraham, Sarah, Isaac. It's not as easy as it looks!

➡ A A S R A B R A H R I S A Z
　　B R A I I G A E T G H A A C
　　B A M F A F H A O R A A L R
　　R M S A R A L M S A R P N Q

And the Livewires still didn't have a name for their dog.

DIARY

Sunday
What would you call the little dog from the beginning of the Bible? Write a few suggestions.

Monday
Can you find out what your name means?

Tuesday
Look back at your list of things that you had been promised. Did you get them all—or did something get forgotten?

Wednesday
Do you ever make promises? Do you sometimes forget them?

Thursday
Did God remember his promises to Abraham?

Friday
Read this little prayer, think about it and then say it...

Saturday
Sarah's baby was a special gift from God. If you were to be given something really special, what would it be? Why?

FOLLOW ABRAHAM'S JOURNEY

> Dear Father, thank you for all the promises that you have made, all the important promises about your people and your world. Help me to learn more about them and about you. Amen

So Tempo had a name, and the Livewires were pleased that Sarah had had a baby—but they were still puzzled about the promises of God. Did Abraham and Sarah have many descendants? Were any of them kings?

The world blinked out and in a whirl of sand and shoes the Livewires landed outside a very grand looking tent. Coming from the tent was a very strange but beautiful sound—music!

Even Tempo was quiet. Through the tent door they could see two hands plucking at the strings of a harp, and strange words met their ears...

Find out about the special way you are created. How tall are you? How heavy are you? What colour is your hair?

You could find out the same things about your family or friends. Make a chart, and include all sorts of things like eye colour and shoe size as well.

God, It seems, knows an awful lot. After all, God knew about Sarah's baby and all those fingerprints. Sometimes there are things that we might not want God to know. If you have some things that you wouldn't like God to know then write them on a bit of paper, or just remember them. You'll need them later.

Surely God can't be everywhere!

The song burst out loud again.

If I flew away beyond the east or lived in the farthest place in the west, you would be there to lead me, you would be there to help me.

PSALM 139:9-10

You see, the singer of the song knows that God is everywhere and that even if you don't want him to he knows all about you, to lead you and guide you...

The Livewires listened to the end of the song...

... guide me in the everlasting way...

Dear God, even though I get things wrong I know that you are always near me. Thank you.

Quartz brushed away a tear, 'That was lovely,' she said.

Take your list and think about the things on it and then say this little prayer.

Throw the list away!

20

The music had stopped and the hands could no longer be seen in the tent. The Livewires waited for the singer to come out but he didn't. The tent door closed and there was silence.

Annie-log could stand it no longer, she typed quickly into Boot's keyboard: 'Who was playing?'

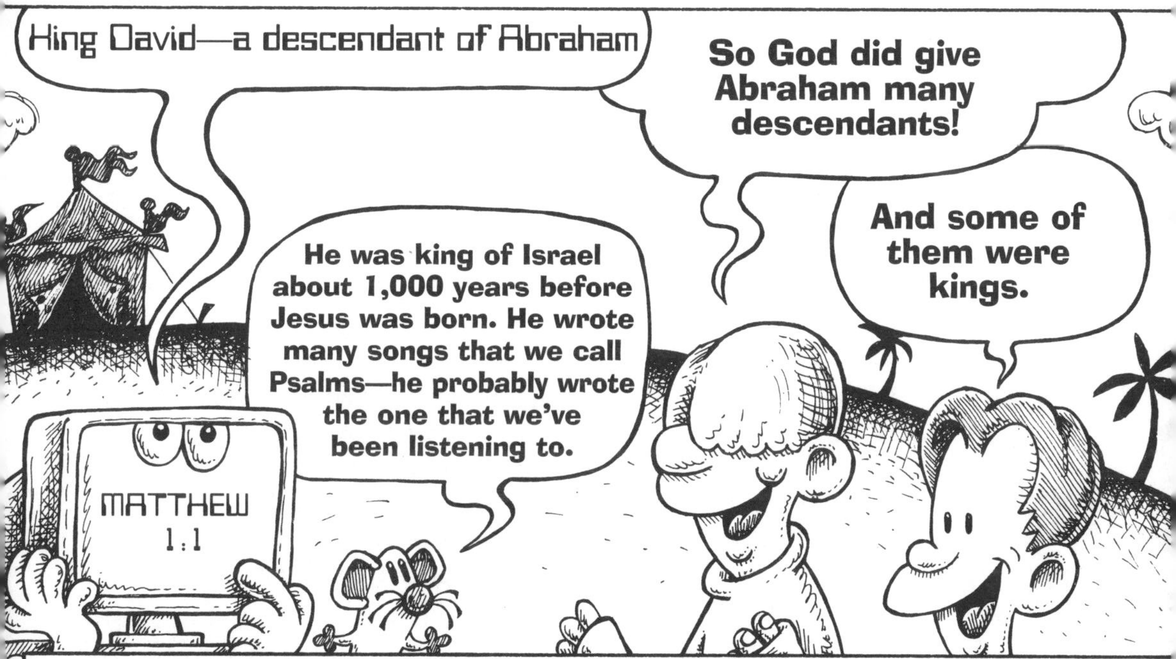

King David—a descendant of Abraham

So God did give Abraham many descendants!

He was king of Israel about 1,000 years before Jesus was born. He wrote many songs that we call Psalms—he probably wrote the one that we've been listening to.

And some of them were kings.

MATTHEW 1:1

It seems that whatever God says happens, even if we laugh like Sarah or are just surprised like Digit. The sun was going down and the Livewires watched it quietly while Boot played back the song—he'd stored it in his memory!

You are all round me on every side; you protect me with your power. Your knowledge of me is too deep; it is beyond my understanding.

PSALM 139:5-6

That sunset looks a bit like a fingerprint...

Yeah, God's fingerprint...

The Livewires have been having an exciting time—but they weren't all happy...

Can't we go to a town? I wanna boogie!

A town? Sure...

'Zechariah... was chosen to burn incense on the altar. So he went into the Temple of the Lord, while the crowd of people outside prayed...'

LUKE 1:9-10

The Livewires found themselves in a jostling crowd of women. They were surrounded by a huge building and everyone was hot. Tempo was nowhere to be seen.

Co-o-l! Well OK it's hot, but where are we?

This is the temple: we Jews worship God here. My husband Zechariah is a priest and is to burn the incense today. I'm very proud of him.

Tape up

Cut off

It is difficult to describe where the Livewires are, the temple is a complicated place. Let's make a model of it. We will start while Quartz talks to Elizabeth. First of all you will need a big tray—use a cereal box; cut the front off.

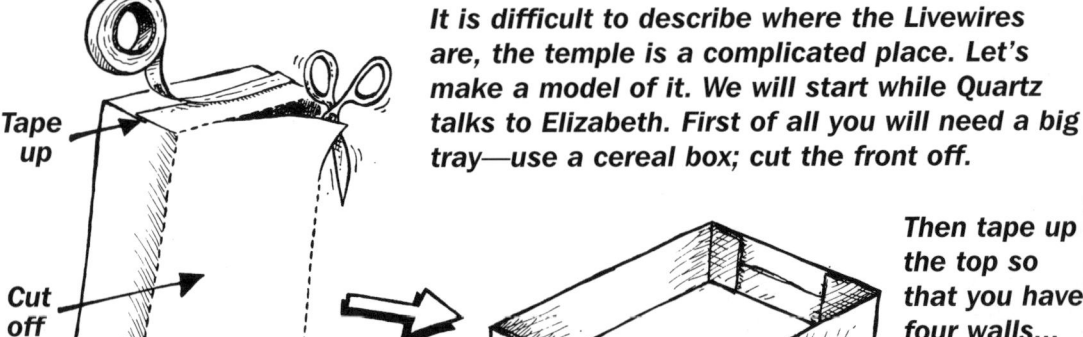

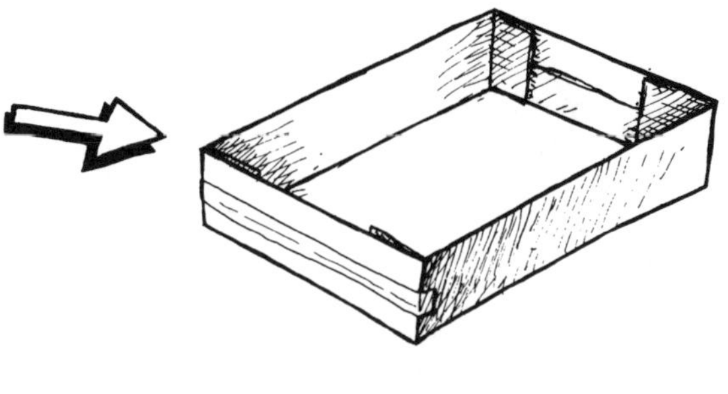

Then tape up the top so that you have four walls...

Elizabeth talked with the Livewires for a long time, she knew all about the stories of creation and about Abraham, and she had a sad story of her own...

And like Sarah you see, I have had no children and I am now far too old.

But Sarah did have a baby...

I know, but we've had no angels or great words from God for many years now. We are all just waiting. One of our prophets, a man called Malachi wrote, 'I will send my messenger to prepare the way for me.' So we are waiting for that to happen.

Elizabeth showed the Livewires round part of the temple. There were lots of pillars and two very big gates; one out of the temple called the Beautiful Gate, and one further in with steps going up to it.

We will add these bits to our model. You will need a smaller box to fit inside your cereal box like this:

Cut Off

Fold here
Cut here
Fold here

Fold back

Glue small box here

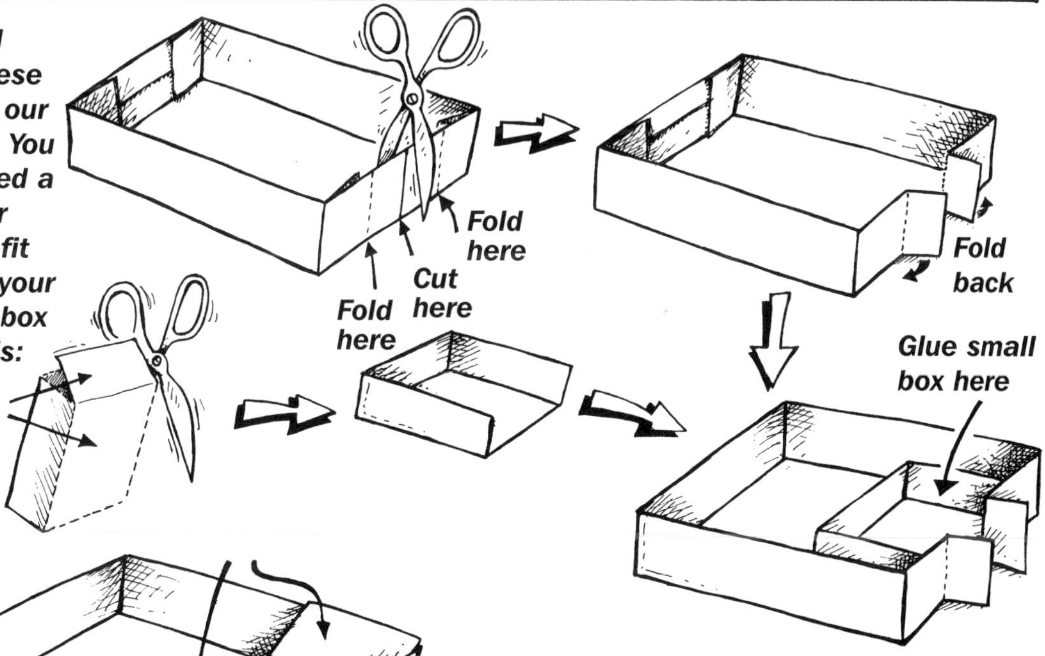

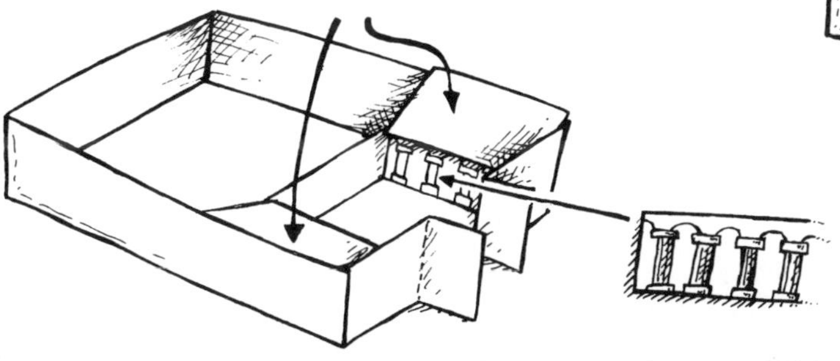

Then put some roofs over the top as the diagram shows. Some of the pillars are drawn to help you.

23

Elizabeth had only been able to show the Livewires around part of the temple because women were not allowed into some parts of it.

Suddenly there was a great noise from inside the gate with the steps up to it.

That's the Court of Israel, where the men go. What has happened?

There was a lot of shouting and pushing then someone came and spoke to Elizabeth, who turned pale and hurried away.

What is going on?

I'll ask Boot.

'...the angel said to him, 'Don't be afraid Zechariah! God has heard your prayer, and your wife Elizabeth will bear you a son. You are to name him John... he will get the Lord's people ready for him...'

LUKE 1:13-17

Digit has heard that somewhere before...

Hey, that is what Malachi wrote! It's what Elizabeth is waiting for.

Look Elizabeth is coming back...

Let's add the next bit to our temple model, the court of Israel, this will need a long box or perhaps the top part of another cereal box across the middle of the tray, like this....

So now we have a Court of Women and a Court of Israel.

Is there anything that you are waiting for that you'd like to happen?

Perhaps you'd like to talk to God about it.

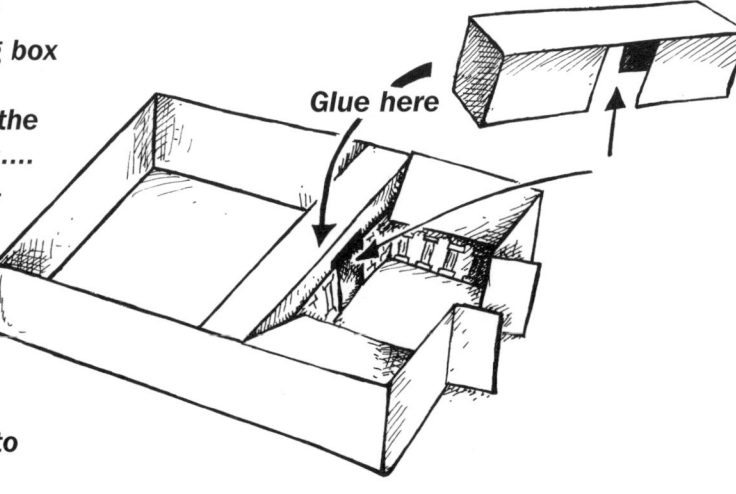

Glue here

24

Elizabeth came rushing back into the Court of Women. The Livewires could hear her telling all her friends what had happened...

Zechariah was in the Holy place burning the incense when an angel called Gabriel appeared and told him that we would have a baby. Well, Zechariah didn't believe the angel and said so! The angel said that because he didn't believe he wouldn't be able to talk until the baby was born. He had to tell me all this with signs because he can't speak.

Is this true, Boot?

LUKE 1:18-23

Elizabeth turned to the Livewires.

If what the angel said is true this could be a great day for all Jewish people.

But we're not Jewish.

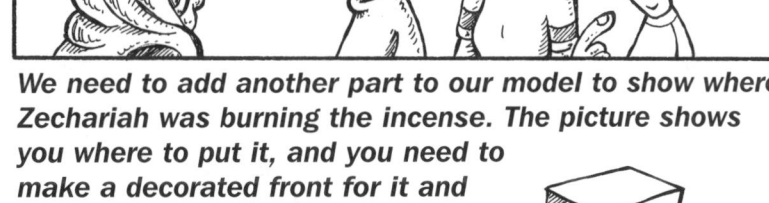

What! You shouldn't be here at all! Quick come with me.

We need to add another part to our model to show where Zechariah was burning the incense. The picture shows you where to put it, and you need to make a decorated front for it and stick it on. Like this...

Glue here

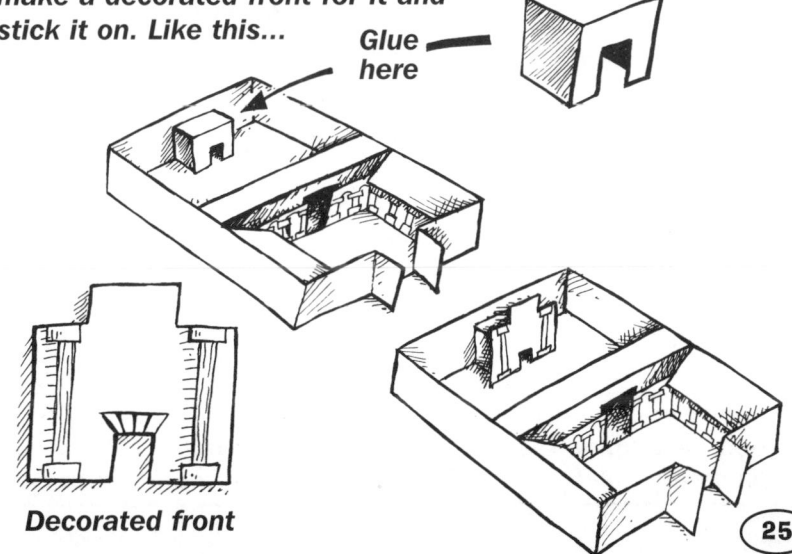

Decorated front

25

Elizabeth had hustled the Livewires to the outer court of the temple. They stood looking around. This bit was the Court of Gentiles and it was full of stalls selling anything you wanted, it was very noisy and smelly! They were soon lost in the crowd and couldn't see Elizabeth anywhere.

A well-known barking sound reached their ears. It was Tempo! Data bent down to greet him and something caught her eye:

Look, a coin in Tempo's footprint. It says 'Augustus'.

He was a Roman Emperor; I know, I did it in history.

Yeah that was 2,000 years ago!

Do you think that Elizabeth does have a baby? I mean, it seems a bit impossible.

Impossible? Haven't you noticed when God says something, it happens!

Some time later... Elizabeth became pregnant. 'Now at last the Lord has helped me,' she said.

LUKE 1:24-25

If you can find a larger piece of card or board you can use it to make the Court of the Gentiles in your model like this:

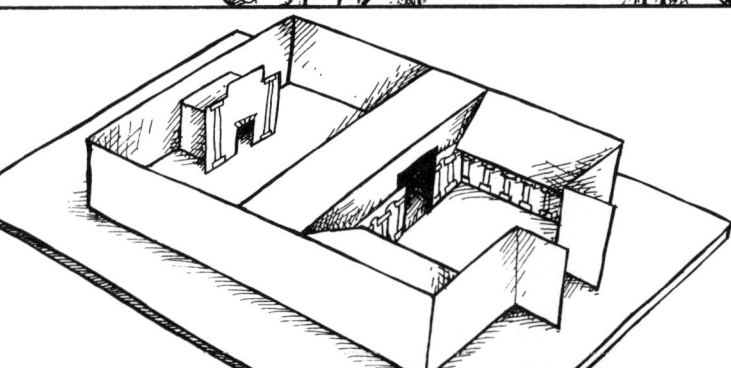

Sometimes things seem impossible or difficult and it is good to remember that God, who made the world, knows how to make things work out. Spend a few moments quietly thinking about this. And then talk to God about it.

Sunday
Spend some time this week making your model temple look really brilliant. You can add pillars and decorations by drawing them on paper and then sticking them on the model.

Monday
The temple was a very special place. Make a list of special buildings that you know.

Tuesday
The temple was used as a place to worship God—how many buildings on your list are places where people meet to worship God?

Wednesday
Can you find out anything about the Roman Emperor Augustus?

Thursday
Do you think that Elizabeth laughed when she was told that she was to have a baby?

Friday
Our Father, thank you for the places that have been made where people can meet to worship you. Be with all the people who meet in those places and help us to see that you can be found anywhere in the world that you made.

Saturday
Make some labels for your model: this plan will help.

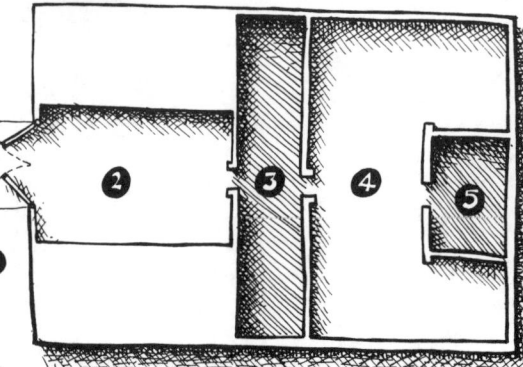

A Map of the Temple

❶ Court of the Gentiles
❷ Court of Women
❸ Court of Israel
❹ Holy place
❺ Holy of Holies

28

Yes it is John. He has been living in the desert and eating what he could find. People came to him from Jerusalem, and all the country near the River Jordan. They confessed their sins, and he baptized them in the river.

That is how he got his nickname 'John the Baptist'.

Water is a strange thing, it is all around us but it is easy to forget. See how many 'water' words you can find in this bucket of letters.

Think how often you use water and then think what it would be like without this very special thing. In a quiet moment you could write a prayer for those people who do not have much water. Write it in the cloud.

The Livewires were amazed. The last time they had seen John he had been a little baby in Elizabeth's arms. Now here he was a grown man about 30 years old!

They went towards his voice and saw a crowd of people listening to him speak as he stood in the river. It was a big crowd. Some were in the water and some on the bank of the river...

Some people asked John:

Colour the picture very carefully to show where all the water is.

The Livewires listened carefully to see what John's answer would be.

'I am "the voice of someone shouting in the desert: Make a straight path for the Lord to travel!"'

JOHN 1:23

John was using the words of the prophet Isaiah and he was using the water to show that people had made a promise; a promise that they would be part of God's people.

Father, help me to remember the promises that I have made and to keep them. Amen.

This was all too weird. Who was the prophet Isaiah?

Isaiah was a very important prophet who lived hundreds of years ago. One of the things he said was that the people of Israel needed to get themselves ready for the coming of God's special servant. Making a 'straight path' was a picture to remind them that they should get everything ready and be prepared.

I'm confused, we didn't do this at school.

I'm not confused— I'm hungry!

No, the people asking questions are the confused ones. They thought that when God's prophet came he would make everything right for them.

Yeah, but John is telling them off 'cos they've not been following God's plan very well. They should have been preparing already...

We've been talking so long that we're all hungry!

What is there to eat?

MATTHEW 3.4

John's food was locusts and wild honey.

Ugh!

Tychi knew that the locusts were probably a kind of bean, but she didn't let on!

Can you think of times when you've got ready for a special occasion? What did you do to prepare for it?

You might like to write about a time that was really important to you—or draw a picture of it.

DIARY

Sunday
Who do you think John was talking about when he said, 'There is the Lamb of God'? J _ _ u _

Monday
Think a bit more about water. You could collect water pictures from magazines or catalogues and make a collage with them.

Tuesday
Have you been baptized? It you have, find out when and where.

Wednesday
John baptized people in the River Jordan. Look on the map to see where the Jordan river is.

Thursday
Which other rivers do you know of: In your country? In the world?

Friday
By being baptized the people were showing that they were part of God's people. How many other groups of people have special signs of belonging?

Saturday

> Father, help me to remember that by being one of your people I am special. Amen.

35

Boot has been getting you to use your senses. He has a bit of time to himself now because the Livewires are asleep!

They've not got much sense!

While the Livewires are asleep, Boot's going to tell you a bit about senses.

Here is a clue to the first sense.

With this sense you can tell what is hot or cold, what is rough or smooth.

Once Jesus was in a town where there was a man who was suffering from a dreaded skin disease. When he saw Jesus, he threw himself down and begged him, 'Sir, if you want to, you can make me clean.'

Jesus stretched out his hand and _ _ _ c _ed him. 'I do want to,' he answered. 'Be clean!' At once the disease left the man.

LUKE 5:12-13

In this story Jesus uses _ _ _ _ _ to heal a man. How do people use _ _ _ _ h to help and heal each other?

Think about it then say this little prayer:

Dear God, thank you for the sense of _o_ _ _. Help me to use your gift of _ _ u_ _ to help other people. Amen

37

Here's the next clue:

You do this one with chocolate, gravy, ice cream, carrots, and chips!

It is difficult to think of t _ _ _ _ being important, but think what it would be like if you couldn't _ a _ _ _ at all. God has made the world full of _ _ _ _ _ s for us to enjoy and if we couldn't _ _ _ _ e we might eat something that was bad for us! Boot has a little story to tell us about _ _ _ t _ .

It is about a time when Jesus was at a wedding and they ran out of wine...

'...six stone water jars were there, each one large enough to hold about a hundred litres. Jesus said to the servants, 'Fill these jars with water.' They filled them to the brim, and then he told them, 'Now draw some water out and take it to the man in charge of the feast.' They took him the water, which had now turned into wine, and he t _ _ _ _ d it... He said to the bridegroom, 'Everyone else serves the best wine first... But you have kept the best wine until now!'

JOHN 2:6-10

Father, thank you for the gift of _ _ s_e. I pray that people without food will be given food because of your love. Amen

Jesus made wine that t _ _ _ _ d better than the other wine bought for the wedding!

Think about God's gift of t_ _t_, and think of those who might be without the chance to use this sense through illness or lack of food.

38

Boot is going to start with his story this time. See if you can work out what the sense is. Remember—we've already had taste and touch...

JOHN 12:1-3

Six days before the Passover, Jesus went to Bethany, the home of Lazarus. They prepared a dinner for him there, which Martha helped to serve; Lazarus was one of those who were sitting at the table with Jesus. Then Mary took half a litre of a very expensive perfume made of pure nard, poured it on Jesus' feet, and wiped them with her hair. The sweet s _ _ _ _ of the perfume filled the whole house.

Nard was very expensive. It comes from a plant that grows in India. You could look India up in an atlas and see how far it would have to travel to reach Israel...

Mary used the perfume to show how important she thought Jesus was.

Different things have different _ m _ _ _s; how many s_ _ _ _ y things are there in your house? Why are they important to you? Make a list. I've started you off with a couple of things.

Soap

Toothpaste

_____

_____

Here is a little prayer to say:

Our Father, you gave us the sense of _ _ e _ l. Help us to use it to find out just how special your world is through the _ m _ _ _ of things like food and flowers. Amen.

39

Here's Boot with a story about the other sense beginning with 'S':

'...some people brought a blind man to Jesus and begged him to touch him. Jesus took the blind man by the hand and led him out of the village. After spitting on the man's eyes, Jesus placed his hands on him and asked him, "Can you see anything?"

The man looked up and said, "Yes, I can see people, but they look like trees walking about."

Jesus again placed his hands on the man's eyes. This time the man looked intently, his eyesight returned, and he saw everything clearly.'

MARK 8:22-25

Think a moment about s _ _ _ _. You can see, you can read this book, but could you tell which was the longest line at the beginning of this unit??

Perhaps you could tell that they were both the same length!

Sometimes we need help to see things. Like the blind man in the story, we need to look twice and have Jesus' help.

Sometimes we dogs say 'see' when we mean understand. We say things like 'Oh now I see it' if we are doing difficult maths and it suddenly makes sense. I wonder if humans do that?

Dear Lord Jesus...

Can you make up your own prayer about _ _ _ h _? Have a go in this space.

40

Hey Boot, it's getting late and we've got one sense left.

We dogs are very good at it!

Yes, dogs are good at it—can you guess what it is? Boot's story will help you.

'Some people brought ... a man who was deaf and could hardly speak, and they begged Jesus to place his hands on him. So Jesus took him off alone, away from the crowd, put his fingers in the man's ears, spat and touched the man's tongue. Then Jesus looked up to heaven... and said to the man... 'Open up'. At once the man was able to hear... and he began to talk without any trouble. All who heard were completely amazed. 'How well he does everything!' they exclaimed. 'He even causes the deaf to hear and the dumb to speak!'

MARK 7:32-37

Sit quietly for a minute and listen to the sounds around you. What can you hear? You could talk to God about one sound that you heard.

Boot has shown you all five senses now. Can you make a senses wordsearch? Add the names of the senses into the spaces of this letter square. Then copy the wordsearch out and show your friends: see if they can find all five!

			A	F	L
P	M				C
H	A	F			
L	P	S	M	T	A	S
Q	R	T			
L	F	G	H	A	G	T
E	N	G	O	I	L	F

SMELL

HEARING

TOUCH

SIGHT

TASTE

41

Sunday
Use one magazine and do a survey. How many adverts are about each sense?
Make a chart like this:

	Sense	Smell	Taste	Sight	Hearing	Touch
Number of Adverts						

Some adverts may use more than one!

Monday
Write a Haiku poem about a sense. (Remember to use the 5 syllables, 7 syllables, 5 syllables pattern.) Here's one about to start you off:
Sound runs into me -
A million tiny feet;
I am hearing rain

Tuesday
Think why God gave us senses. Write your ideas down here.

Wednesday
Which sense do you like best? Do you like looking at pictures (sight), hearing music, cuddling a teddy (touch) or maybe eating (taste)?

Thursday
Think how it would be to be without a sense. Then say this prayer:

Dear Lord, thank you for the senses that I have, help me to use them wisely. And be with those who are not able to use all of the senses. Amen

Friday
You've already made up a prayer for sight. Now try and make a prayer about all the senses.

Saturday
Look through some magazines and find adverts that are about one of the senses like food adverts (taste) or music (hearing). Cut them out and keep them.

The Livewires woke up slowly. They were sore from lying on the ground. Tim was nearly the last to wake up and he was hungry.

Where can we find breakfast?

Ask Boot to look for breakfast

Tim typed 'Luke for brekfast' into Boot...

You don't spell 'look' like that!

It was too late. Everything blinked out and the Livewires found themselves whizzing through the air and out over the sea. As the travelled they got lower and lower. They sped past a sea port and along a river, almost touching the water. Suddenly they arrived at a town and landed in an untidy heap at the bottom of a stone staircase. A voice came from the top of the steps...

What's all that noise?

Tempo ran up the stairs, barking loudly.

WOOF!

Come on! We'd better follow!

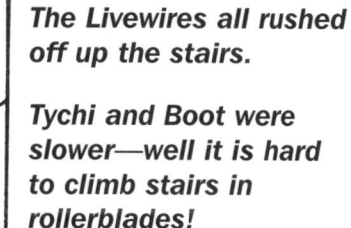

The Livewires all rushed off up the stairs.

Tychi and Boot were slower—well it is hard to climb stairs in rollerblades!

Who have you brought us to anyway?

Luke, our dear doctor...

The doctor's! For breakfast! And all because of a spelling mistake!

COLOSSIANS 4:14

Did you know that breakfast time is a good time for praying? It starts the day off with God. Here is a breakfast prayer:

Dear Lord, I praise you for this new day, for all the things I'm going to do, for the food I'm going to eat and the people I'm going to meet. Amen

(43)

Luke welcomed the Livewires into his rooms.

What a mess, it's like Digit's room back home.

Sorry about all the letters and things. Here—do sit down.

The Livewires sat down in the space Luke had cleared for them.

I'm writing to my friend Theophilus about Jesus. As I am getting old I thought I would write down everything that I have found out about him over the years. All these letters and scrolls have bits about Jesus' life in them. This one is about when Mary found out from the angel Gabriel that she was going to have a baby...

God sent the angel Gabriel to a town in Galilee named Nazareth. He had a message for a young woman promised in marriage to a man named Joseph, who was a descendant of King David. Her name was Mary. The angel said to her, 'Don't be afraid, Mary; God has been gracious to you. You will become pregnant and give birth to a son...'

LUKE 1:26-31

Data had found a folding wooden tablet. Each piece of wood had a space filled with hard wax. She was looking at some marks in the wax through her magnifying glass.

What is this?

It's for writing on, you write into the wax with a sharp pen, or stylus—like this...

Luke showed them how to make marks in the wax and then closed up the writing table.

You could make your own scrolls by glueing lengths of paper to cardboard tubes. You could make several and write some of the Bible stories that you have been learning onto them. (Write the story before you glue the scroll together.)

44

This is a scroll which was written by Matthew—it's in his book about Jesus—and it's about how Joseph, who was engaged to Mary, was told by God about Mary having a baby.

An angel of the Lord appeared to him in a dream and said, 'Joseph, descendant of David, do not be afraid to take Mary to be your wife. For it is by the Holy Spirit that she has conceived. She will have a son, and you will name him Jesus—because he will save his people...'

MATTHEW 1:20-21

Does that mean that Jesus' name means something then?

Yeah, like Isaac meant 'laughter'

Oh yes, Jesus is a very old name. It is the Jewish name Joshua but it is written 'Jesus' in Greek. I'm writing all my book in Greek because that is the language that most people understand around here. Jesus means 'God saves'.

The very first Christians had a special sign which they used to show that they believed in Jesus. It was a fish! This was because the word for fish in Greek is ΙΧΘΥΣ *(you say 'ichthus') and the Christians made an 'acrostic' from it like this:*

Letter	Greek word	English letter	English word
Ι	ΙΕΣΟΥΣ	I	Jesus
Χ	ΧΡΙΣΤΟΣ	CH	Christ
Θ	ΘΕΟΥ	TH	God's
Υ	ΥΙΟΣ	U	Son
Σ	ΣΟΤΕΡ	S	Saviour

It's all Greek to me!

Isn't that clever?

You could make your own 'fish' sign or badge and write the Greek letters in it.

The Livewires had been listening carefully to Luke for a long time when Tim suddenly remembered why they had ended up with Luke in the first place.

Breakfast!

What did you say?

Breakfast! That's what we came here for, and we've not had any yet...

They got up and followed Luke out into the sun. Tychi and Boot stayed behind, it would have been a long walk for a computer! Following Luke, the Livewires went down the steps and then along the road which itself went down towards the river. Soon they found themselves in a market full of bustle and noise. Tempo rushed about very excited, there were so many things to smell!

Luke bought fruit, bread, and some fish. He led them away from the market, past the amphitheatre; as they walked back to his house Luke told them what he had learnt about Mary.

Sniff! Sniff!

Mary was surprised by the arrival of the angel Gabriel, but she knew enough about her own people—the Jewish people—to know that God had sent angels in the past, and that special babies had been born. She remembered the stories of Sarah and Hannah. Mary knew that God's plan had worked out well for those who had obeyed God's messages—she remembered the stories of Abraham and Moses...

They had arrived back at Luke's rooms by now, and there was Boot—he must have been listening to Luke as he came in!

'I am the Lord's servant,' said Mary, 'may it happen to me as you have said.'

LUKE 1:38

Before they ate Luke said a prayer to ask God to bless the food, then he broke the bread up and shared it round.

Then they were silent for a while whilst they ate and drank.

Can you remember any times when special things have happened to you? How did you feel about it?

Everyone was feeling comfortable now, though Tim and Tempo were still eating.

This is one of my favourite stories from the beginning of my book. It is about a time when Mary went to see her cousin Elizabeth...

We saw her—she's John's mum.

Yes that's right and when Mary went to see Elizabeth she was pregnant with John. Here's the story...

Luke started to read from a scroll. Boot knows the story as well, so we'll let him tell us.

Mary got ready and hurried off to a town in the hill country of Judea. She went into Zechariah's house and greeted Elizabeth. When Elizabeth heard Mary's greeting, the baby moved within her. Elizabeth was filled with the Holy Spirit and said in a loud voice, 'You are the most blessed of all women, and blessed is the child you will bear!... as soon as I heard your greeting, the baby within me jumped with gladness. How happy you are to believe that the Lord's message to you will come true.'

LUKE 1.39-45

So John and Jesus were related, that's cool.

Can you find the road which will take Mary to Elizabeth?

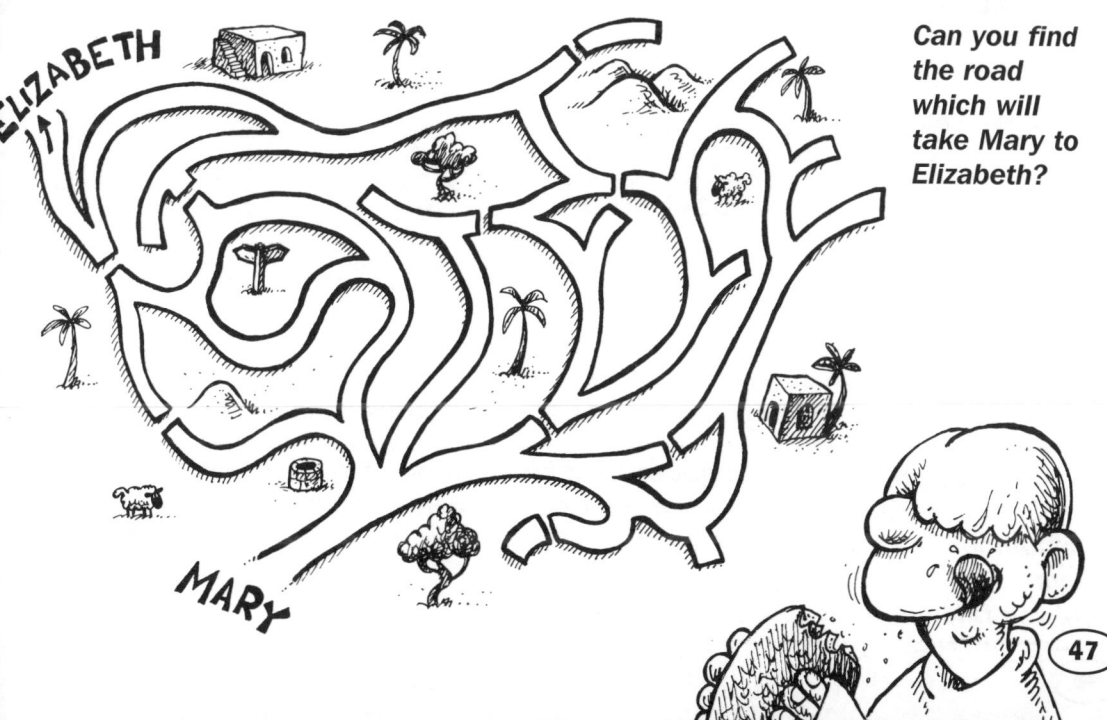

ELIZABETH

MARY

47

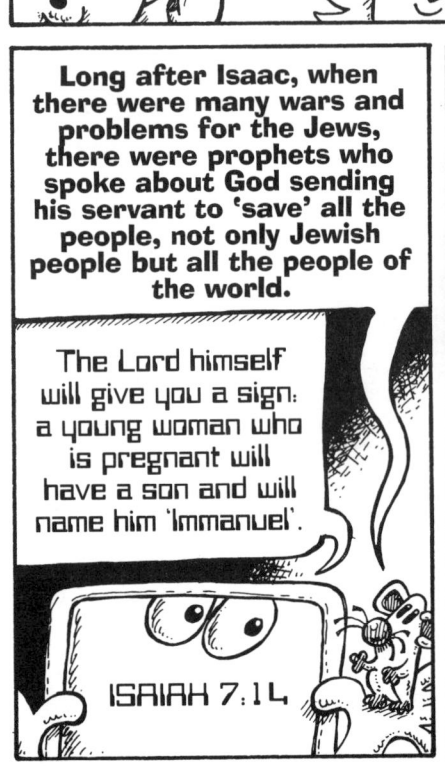

Something is puzzling me. Why was Mary's baby so important?

It's a bit like Isaac again, God said it was going to happen, so it did.

scratch!

Yes, it is a bit like Isaac. Without Sarah having Isaac, God would not have been able to complete his promise to Abraham.

Er... yeah.

The promise about lots of descendants, yeah?

Long after Isaac, when there were many wars and problems for the Jews, there were prophets who spoke about God sending his servant to 'save' all the people, not only Jewish people but all the people of the world.

The Lord himself will give you a sign: a young woman who is pregnant will have a son and will name him 'Immanuel'.

ISAIAH 7:14

Another baby?

No, we think about Jesus when we read Isaiah's words.

'... he will be called Immanuel' (which means, 'God is with us').

So Jesus' name means 'God saves' and 'God is with us'? That's amazing!

MATTHEW 1:23

Luke agreed that this was amazing.

Luke told the Livewires that it had been nice to have had their company for breakfast, but now he really did have to get on with his book.

So the Livewires left Luke to get on with his work. As they walked out into the sunshine they chatted about what their names meant. They made their way to the amphitheatre, where they sat down to eat the lunch Luke had kindly packed for them.
Did you find out what your name means?

48

DIARY

Sunday
Beginnings are good times for prayers but endings are good too. They are very good for thank you prayers.

Monday
You have already written a prayer for the beginning of a day. Try making up a prayer for the beginning of the week.

Tuesday
What is the best bit of good news you have ever heard?

Wednesday
Why do you think Mary believed what the angel told her? What happened to Zechariah who didn't believe the angel?

Thursday
The Ichthus fish is a clever symbol. Do you know any other Christian symbols? Make a little list of them...

Friday
What do you like best for breakfast?

Saturday
When Mary heard the news from the angel she went to see her cousin Elizabeth. What do you do when you hear exciting news?

> Dear Father, thank you for all the things I have done this week. The stories I have read, the things I have learned, the food that I have eaten and the people that I have met. Amen

Why did Abraham leave his family?

Why did Zechariah name his son John?

Why are there people in the world?

The Livewires were a bit confused. They had seen lots of things but they had not worked out why they had happened. And their heads were full of questions. Annie-log decided to type 'HELP!' on Boot's keyboard.

Boot's screen seemed to go crazy! All sorts of messages flashed up, the Livewires could only catch a few of them.

The Lord said to Abraham...

GENESIS 12:1

I am Gabriel... God... sent me to speak to you and tell you...

LUKE 1:19

Then God said, 'And now we will make human beings...'

GENESIS 1:26

Boot looked very pleased and gave a little bleep.

Hang on a minute! Boot's telling us that God speaks!

What did we keep hearing when Boot showed us the story of creation?

A V _ _ _ _ !

50

What else did God say, Boot?

C:\> PLEASE WAIT...

God created human beings... he created them male and female, blessed them, and said, 'Have many children, so that your descendants will live all over the earth and bring it under their control. I am putting you in charge of the fish, the birds, and all the wild animals.'

GENESIS 1:27-28

I wonder what that means?

It means that we can do what we like!

The Livewires don't all agree.

It means that we should care for all animals, and not eat any meat!

It means that we should try to look after animals—but not the nasty ones, like spiders!

No. We can eat meat but we mustn't be cruel, like shutting animals in the dark and stuff!

Do you think that Digit is right? YES NO

What do you think? Write it in the empty bubble and draw yourself in the head shape.

51

The Livewires had followed Sarah and Abraham for hundreds of miles because of something that God said.

It was part of God's big plan for Abraham and Sarah to have a baby whose grandchildren would be the founders of twelve famous tribes, the twelve tribes of Israel, but that's another adventure.

So God's got a plan then?

Well you can't go around making promises unless you plan to keep them!

You mean like 'Sarah will have a baby?'

Yeah, like that

We've heard so much about promises that I've forgotten what God said to Abraham!

The Lord took him outside and said, 'Look at the sky and try to count the stars; you will have as many descendants as that.'

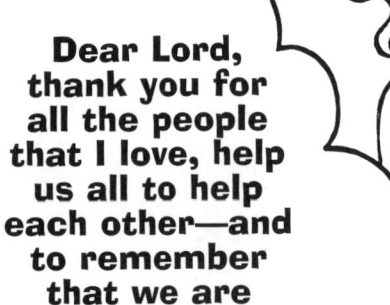

GENESIS 15:5

Children and families were very important then, people got very worried about the family continuing. I know, I did it at school!

Dear Lord, thank you for all the people that I love, help us all to help each other—and to remember that we are part of your family.

Families can be very different. Can you think of some ways in which they might be important?

52

So Elizabeth's baby was part of God's plan?

John!

So John's life had a purpose—God wanted him to get things ready for Jesus, didn't he?

God sent his messenger, a man named John, who came to tell people about the light, so that all should hear the message and believe.

JOHN 1:6-7

What is the light?

Jesus said, 'I am the light of the world... Whoever follows me will have the light of life and will never walk in darkness.'

JOHN 8:12

A light is something that shows us the way. We live in a world of difficult choices. Jesus came to show us the way God wants us to live. You see, Jesus' life had a purpose too—to give us a way to God

Here is a 'light maze'—can you guide the candle to the flame in the middle of the maze?

You could make up mazes of your own, guide the torch to the bulb, guide the plug to the socket...

53

So...

Why did Abraham leave his family?—because in God's plan Abraham's life had a purpose, and God told him so.

Why did Zechariah name his son John?—because in God's plan John's life had a purpose, and God told Zechariah so.

Why are there people in the world?—because in God's plan all of us have a purpose.

What has God told us?

Nothing!

I'm not so sure...

Well, what about the voice in the creation story?

That's where I came in!

The Livewires were puzzled by the question, 'What has God told us?'

They knew that God had spoken to Abraham and Zechariah, and used angels and prophets, but they couldn't say whether God had spoken to them. Then Little Ben had a good idea...

Hey Boot! Has God told us anything?

Yeah, has he spoken to us?

We thought you'd never ask!!!

In the past, God spoke to our ancestors many times and in many ways through the prophets, but in these last days he has spoken to us through his Son. He is the one through whom God created the universe...

HEBREWS 1:1-2

What is the name of God's Son? Can you remember what it means?

_ _ S _ _

Annie-log typed at Boot's keyboard, with no success until suddenly...

So what has God said then, through his Son?

I'll ask.

Jesus drew near and said to them, 'I have been given all authority in heaven and on earth. Go, then, to all peoples everywhere and make them my disciples: baptize them in the name of the Father, the Son, and the Holy Spirit, and teach them to obey everything I have commanded you. And I will be with you always, to the end of the age.'

MATTHEW 28:18

So... if God has told us this—it means...

... that we are going to have to find out what it was that Jesus commanded!

I think they'll have to get a Bible.

I know—when we get back we'll put our pocket money together and buy a Bible!

Told you so!

Commands are special things—what sorts of people give commands?
Make a list:

Soldiers _____ _____

_____ _____ _____

_____ _____

_____

Did you notice that God 'commanded' at the beginning of the Livewires' adventure?

I did, that's why I'm here...

55

DIARY

Sunday
Abraham was sent to look at the stars. Have you ever tried to count them?

Monday
You could find out more about the stars, God made them too!

Tuesday
A difficult one—can you make a list of all the prophets that the Livewires have heard about in this adventure?

I_____   M_____   E_____

Wednesday
Do you know the names any other prophets?

Thursday
Dear Lord, thank you for all those people who have spoken the words that you wanted them to say, the Old Testament prophets, John the Baptist and especially for Jesus. Amen

Friday
John the Baptist had a job to do when he grew up. What do you want to do when you grow up?

Saturday

Our Father, you have given us all choices to make as we grow. Help us in the big things we choose, and the little things. Amen

It seems ages since the power cut in Annie-log's bedroom, and something tells me that the adventure is coming to an end.

Some mouse you mean, if Boot doesn't get back soon his batteries will run out!

But we can't go yet— I want to find out about Mary's baby, Jesus.

Yeah, Luke was so sure that he was a special baby.

LUKE 1.46 & 54-55

O.K. One last time!

Whoosh. They all spun out of control again. While they spun they could all hear a woman's voice singing:

♪ **My heart praises the Lord; He has kept the promise he made to our ancestors, and has come to the help of his servant Israel. He has remembered to show mercy to Abraham and to all his descendants for ever.** ♪

The Livewires dropped into an untidy pile just in time to see two ladies disappear into a house.

Can you guess who the two ladies are?

Here are some clues:

They are both going to have babies. They were both promised babies by an angel called Gabriel.

A

Can you fill in their names?

57

Where are we?

Back at the time of John the Baptist, I think. Look, there's another coin with 'Augustus' on it.

Perhaps that was Mary singing.

I wonder what she was singing about?

Emperor Augustus ordered a census to be taken throughout the Roman Empire. Everyone, then, went to register himself, each to his own town. Joseph went from the town of Nazareth... to the town of Bethlehem... the birthplace of King David. Joseph went there because he was a descendant of David. He went to register with Mary...

LUKE 2:1-5

Mary had been singing because she realized that God was remembering the promise that he had made to Abraham all those years before. Remind us Boot.

....I will give you many descendants and they will become a great nation... And through you I will bless all the nations.

GENESIS 12:2-3

Father, it is good to be able to fulfil our promises. Help us always to be grateful to others who fulfil their promises. Amen.

How do you feel when something happens that you have been promised? A present, a trip out...

How do you feel when you do something that you promised to do? Good? Happy?

Let's go to Bethlehem then, and see what's going on.

While they were in Bethlehem, the time came for her to have her baby. She gave birth to her first son, wrapped him in strips of cloth and laid him in a manger...

LUKE 2:6-7

Even I know that bit... OOOPS

And the Livewires were off again, spinning through time...

Draw a picture of what you think it might have been like when Jesus was born. You could draw him in a manger in a stable with Mary and Joseph. Do you think that anyone else might have been there? The innkeeper or his wife perhaps?

Bethlehem was packed with people. All of them were far too busy to notice six kids wandering about.
Even if they did have a dog and a rollerblading computer with them!
It got darker and colder—night was drawing in.
The Livewires tried to find a place to stay, but every inn and house was full!

Isn't this what happened to Mary and Joseph?

Yes it is. I did it at school!

That's right. That's why they put the baby in a manger...

Dear Father, there are many people in our world with nowhere to go. Be with them and with their families, and help them to find a place to live and grow.

There was no room for them to stay in the inn.

LUKE 2:7

59

The Livewires were suddenly startled by a terrible noise!
There was a group of men and boys running and jumping, shouting and singing in the middle of the night.
Tempo started to bark at them, they stopped...

Who are you?

We're shepherds— from the hills..

Why are you making so much noise?

'Cos of the angel. He told us to go and find a baby so we did!

I'll type 'shepherds'

There were some shepherds... spending the night in the fields. An angel of the Lord appeared to them... the angel said to them, '... I am here with good news for you, which will bring great joy to all the people. This very day in David's town your Saviour was born—Christ the Lord...' Suddenly a great army of heaven's angels appeared... singing... 'Glory to God in the highest heaven...'

LUKE 2:8-14

The shepherds dashed off back to their sheep. Can you find a path that will allow them to gather all the sheep up on the way back? Don't cross paths or use the same path twice!

The Livewires watched them go. They were very tired. Even the stone doorstep of the over-full inn looked comfortable so, in a weary heap, they huddled up together and soon fell asleep...

60

While they're all asleep I'll move us on a bit! That'll surprise 'em.

Tychi flicked through some menus and whoosh... the Livewires were lying in the dust on an open road.

Boot was not pleased

What on earth?...

Hang on I think I've found something. Yes—tracks, look. There's people's shoes and some big animal ones. And look—another coin. But it's not like the Augustus ones.

I'll disable her driver!

WHUMP!

It must have been dropped by someone from another place.

Well if Augustus comes from Rome...

That's west of here, I know, I did it at school. So whoever dropped this must have come from the east!

Some men came from the east to Jerusalem and asked 'Where is the baby born to be the king of the Jews? We saw his star when it came up in the east...' When King Herod heard about this, he was very upset... he sent them to Bethlehem with these instructions: 'Go and make a careful search for the child, and when you find him, let me know, so that I too may go and worship him...'

MATTHEW 2:1-8

Make a list of all the characters that you have heard of in the story of Jesus' birth, you'll need it on the diary page. I've started you off....

Angel _____ _____

Shepherds _____ _____

Joseph _____ _____

_____ _____ _____

_____ _____ _____

(61)

Did the kings go back to Herod? I didn't like the sound of him.

They left, and on their way they saw the same star they had seen in the east... It went ahead of them until it stopped over the place where the child was. They went into the house, and... they brought out their gifts of gold, frankincense and myrrh. Then they returned to their own country by another road, since God had warned them in a dream not to go back to Herod.

MATTHEW 2:9-12

So Herod is jealous!

Isn't it dark? I can hear funny noises.

Tim was right. They could see a couple of shadowy figures walking quickly to the gate of the town, and from behind them came the sound of clanking metal...

I can smell soldiers!

The Lord appeared in a dream to Joseph and said, 'Herod will be looking for the child... get up, take the child and his mother and escape to Egypt...'

MATTHEW 2:13

Tempo began to growl quietly and sniffed around the street. There were two sets of footprints in the dust; one was of two pairs of feet, one big and one small...

A man and a woman I bet.

It must be Mary and Joseph running away.

Joseph's dream was very important, he was able to take Mary and Jesus away before the soldiers found them. (In the second Livewires book you can read about another Joseph who has important dreams.)

62

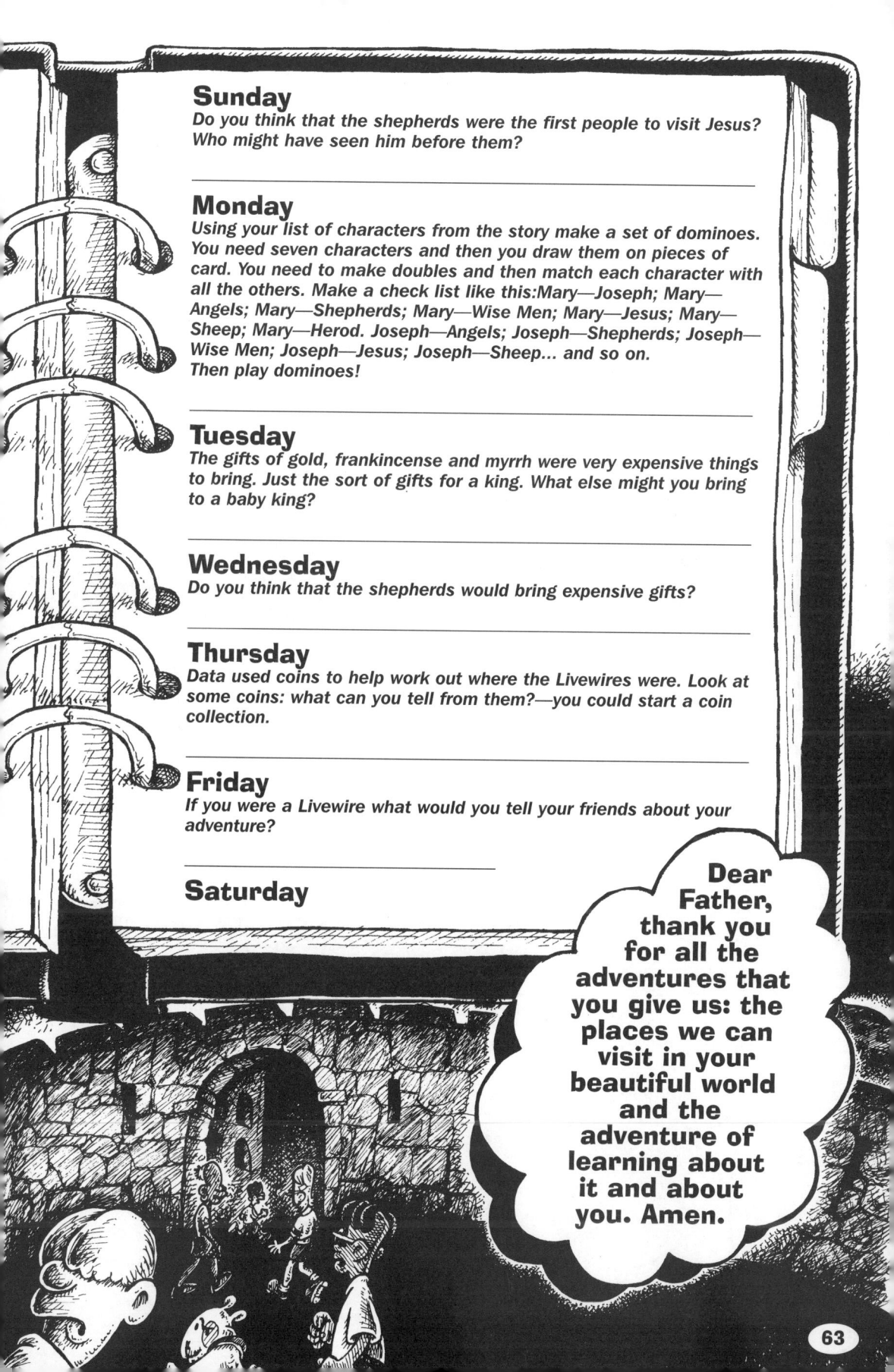

Sunday
Do you think that the shepherds were the first people to visit Jesus? Who might have seen him before them?

Monday
*Using your list of characters from the story make a set of dominoes. You need seven characters and then you draw them on pieces of card. You need to make doubles and then match each character with all the others. Make a check list like this: Mary—Joseph; Mary—Angels; Mary—Shepherds; Mary—Wise Men; Mary—Jesus; Mary—Sheep; Mary—Herod. Joseph—Angels; Joseph—Shepherds; Joseph—Wise Men; Joseph—Jesus; Joseph—Sheep... and so on.
Then play dominoes!*

Tuesday
The gifts of gold, frankincense and myrrh were very expensive things to bring. Just the sort of gifts for a king. What else might you bring to a baby king?

Wednesday
Do you think that the shepherds would bring expensive gifts?

Thursday
Data used coins to help work out where the Livewires were. Look at some coins: what can you tell from them?—you could start a coin collection.

Friday
If you were a Livewire what would you tell your friends about your adventure?

Saturday

> Dear Father, thank you for all the adventures that you give us: the places we can visit in your beautiful world and the adventure of learning about it and about you. Amen.

63

I'm very cold, I wish I was at home.

Tempo's growls became louder, and Annie-log bustled them all under an arch where they crouched down. Shadows of soldiers moved across the wall opposite to them.
Ben was right, it was very cold. Even Tychi's teeth had begun to chatter!
'C... c... c... c'mon Boot.' she said.

The soldiers appeared in the arch. Sharp grains of dust from their footsteps made a cloud round the Livewires. One of the soldiers stood on Tim's fingers and he coughed and spluttered with pain. The clanking stopped, the soldiers turned...

C:\ >Home? Please wait...

In the dark Annie-log reached out and touched Boot's escape key...

Nothing seemed to change, it was still dark and quite cold. The Livewires stayed quite still and held their breath. There was silence. Suddenly the quiet was broken by a cry from Little Ben. 'I can feel the bed!' he said. Boot's screen shone white in the dark and suddenly the lights came back on—the power cut was over. The Livewires pinched themselves to see if they were awake, to see if they had only been dreaming. 'I don't know if we've been dreaming,' said Quartz, 'but we're going to have to decide who looks after this dog!'